W9-BNV-401

Countries Around the World

Scotland

Melanie Waldron

Heinemann Library
Chicago, Illinois

www.heinemannraintree.com
Visit our website to find out
more information about
Heinemann-Raintree books.

To order:

☎ Phone 888-454-2279
🖳 Visit www.heinemannraintree.com
to browse our catalog and order online.

© 2012 Heinemann Library
an imprint of Capstone Global Library, LLC
Chicago, Illinois

All rights reserved. No part of this publication may be reproduced
or transmitted in any form or by any means, electronic or
mechanical, including photocopying, recording, taping, or any
information storage and retrieval system, without permission in
writing from the publisher.

Edited by Louise Galpine, Kate DeVilliers, and Laura Knowles
Designed by Richard Parker
Original illustrations © Capstone Global Library Ltd 2011
Illustrated by Oxford Designers & Illustrators
Picture research by Liz Alexander
Originated by Capstone Global Library Ltd
Printed in China by CTPS

15 14 13 12 11
10 9 8 7 6 5 4 3 2 1

Library of Congress Cataloging-in-Publication Data
Waldron, Melanie.
  Scotland / Melanie Waldron.
    p. cm.—(Countries around the world)
  Includes bibliographical references and index.
  ISBN 978-1-4329-5216-7 (hc)—ISBN 978-1-4329-5241-9 (pb) 1.
Scotland—Juvenile literature. I. Title.
  DA762.W35 2012
  941.1—dc22
                         2010044776

Acknowledgments
We would like to thank the following for permission to reproduce
photographs: Alamy pp. **13** (© Banana Pancake), **17** (© Wig
Worland), **19** (© Roger Covey), **23** (© david tipling), **26** (© tom
Kidd); © AWS Ocean Energy Ltd p. **36**; Corbis pp. **5** (© Ocean),
11 (© David Moir/Reuters); iStockphoto p. **25** (© Chris Hepburn);
Photolibrary pp. **22** (John Tomkins), **29** (epa), **33** (Paul Harris);
Press Association Images p. **32** (Lynne Cameron/PA Archive);
Shutterstock pp. **9** (© TTphoto), **15** (© Yvan), **18** (© John A
Cameron), **21** (© Sue Robinson), **20** (© Ian McDonald), **31**
(© Morag Fleming), **35** (© Robert Anthony), **34** (© Paul Cowan),
46 (© Gary Blakeley), **37** (© Aga & Tomek Adameczek).

Cover photograph of a street entertainer walking the tightrope
at the Edinburgh festival reproduced with permission of Alamy/
© John McKenna.

We would like to thank Rob Bowden for his invaluable help in the
preparation of this book.

Every effort has been made to contact copyright holders of material
reproduced in this book. Any omissions will be rectified in
subsequent printings if notice is given to the publisher.

Disclaimer
All the Internet addresses (URLs) given in this book were valid at
the time of going to press. However, due to the dynamic nature of
the Internet, some addresses may have changed, or sites may have
changed or ceased to exist since publication. While the author
and publisher regret any inconvenience this may cause readers, no
responsibility for any such changes can be accepted by either the
author or the publisher.

Contents

Some words are printed in bold, **like this**. You can find out what they mean by looking in the glossary.

Introducing Scotland

What comes into your mind when you think of Scotland? Do you think of mountains and misty moors, **bagpipes**, and **haggis**? Or do you think of beautiful, vibrant cities and a modern mix of people? Well, both images are correct. Scotland is a unique country with a strong sense of belonging.

Scotland is one of the four countries, along with England, Wales, and Northern Ireland, that make up the United Kingdom (UK). Scotland is the northernmost country of the UK, located in the northwest corner of Europe. However, Scotland has not always been part of the UK. For many centuries Scotland was an independent nation, with an uneasy relationship with England.

The land and the people

Large parts of Scotland are wilderness, with huge mountain ranges and moorlands creating a wonderful sense of space. The islands along the western coast add to the beauty of the landscape. Here you can find beautiful white sandy beaches alongside stark mountain cliffs.

The varying landscape and the history of Scotland have created a lasting and distinct **culture**. Scottish people are very proud of their country and have a strong sense of Scottishness. However, Scots are also happy to welcome new cultures into Scotland, to move forward together in the 21st century.

How to say...

Most Scottish people speak English. The ancient language of Gaelic is spoken by fewer than 2 percent of the population. It is common only in the northwest. Scots is another ancient language, and today many Scottish people still use some Scots words.

Gaelic:	Scotland	*Alba*	**Scots:**	mountain	*ben*
	mountain	*beinn*		beautiful	*bonny*

Eilean Donan Castle has been described as the most beautiful castle in Scotland. It sits on the northwest coast where three lochs (lakes) join, and looks outward toward the island of Skye.

History: A People United

Before Scotland came together as a nation, **Celtic tribes** called Picts lived on the land. At this time Scotland was known as Caledonia. The Picts kept the Romans out, so Caledonia never became part of the Roman Empire.

The Scotti invade

In the 6th century, Irish Celts called Scotti started invading the west coast of Caledonia. The Scotti and the Picts were united under Kenneth MacAlpin in 843 CE. However, it was not until King Malcolm II defeated the **Anglo-Saxons** in the south, around 1018, that Scotland was born.

Invaders!

In the 700s CE, Vikings began to invade from the north. They killed villagers before taking anything of value. The Vikings took control of some areas, before finally giving all the land back between 1232 and 1469.

The Wars of Independence

King Edward I of England invaded Scotland in 1296. This angered the Scots, who came together to resist him. The English were defeated in 1297 at Stirling Bridge. The fighting carried on for over 300 years. One famous battle was in 1314, when Robert the Bruce led the Scots to victory at Bannockburn.

SIR WILLIAM WALLACE (c.1270-1305)

Wallace was a strong leader who united the Scots against Edward I. His army killed 5,000 English troops at Stirling Bridge. Wallace was eventually captured and brutally killed by the English in 1305. The Wallace Monument near Stirling was built to remember him.

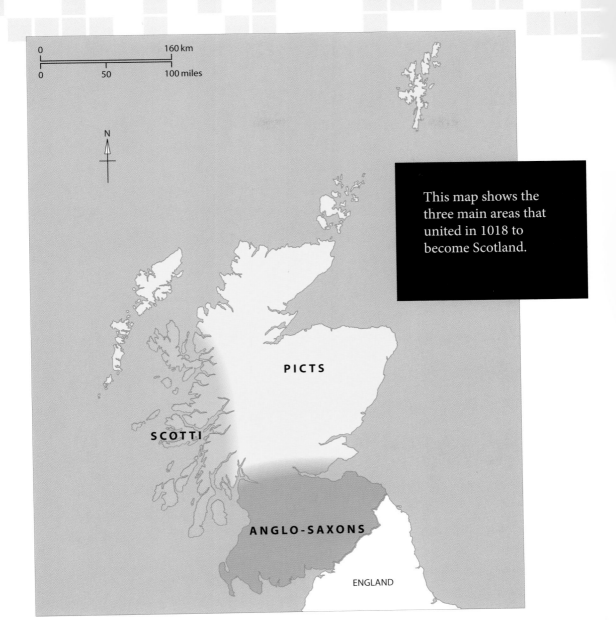

This map shows the three main areas that united in 1018 to become Scotland.

PICTS

SCOTTI

ANGLO-SAXONS

ENGLAND

0   160 km

0   50   100 miles

N

Risings and revolution

From 1603 Scotland and England were ruled by one king or queen, although the two countries were separate. By the end of the 1600s, civil war had ruined Scotland's **economy**, and people were dying from **famine**. Scotland's powerful **nobles** knew joining with England was the only solution. In 1707 the Treaty of Union was signed, and the United Kingdom was born.

Jacobite risings

Many **Highland** Scots wanted the **Catholic** descendants of James I to rule again, instead of the **Protestant** monarchy (king or queen) that was in place in the 1700s. These rebels, called Jacobites, included Charles Edward Stuart. He was also known as "Bonnie Prince Charlie." With his army, he marched as far south as Derby in England. However, he retreated and was finally defeated at the Battle of Culloden in 1746.

The Highland Clearances

During the late 1700s and early 1800s, landowners in the north and west realized that sheep farming would bring them a lot of money. So they began to force **tenants** to leave their land. The Highland Clearances made up to 100,000 people homeless. Some went to live by the coast, to make a living from the sea. Others fled to cities in search of work. Thousands **emigrated** to places such as Canada, the United States, Australia, and New Zealand.

The Industrial Revolution

While the Clearances were a dark time in the Highlands, the Scottish Lowlands were flourishing. During the **Industrial Revolution**, Scotland became a leading **industrialized** country. Steam power led to big advances in **manufacturing**. Large-scale railroad building meant that goods could travel long distances. Glasgow became a world center for shipbuilding. Many people flocked to the cities to find work, so while the Highlands were losing people, the cities were growing rapidly.

Daily life

In the late 1700s and early 1800s, most people who moved to Glasgow ended up living in tenements (blocks of apartments). For the poorest people, these apartments were often squalid and very cramped. Many had only one or two rooms for entire families. Nearly half of all children died before reaching their fifth birthday.

The Forth Rail Bridge was finally completed in 1890. It is over 1.5 miles (2.5 kilometers) long. Up to 4,000 men worked on the bridge, and 57 men were killed during its construction.

Into the 21st century

Events in the 1900s left many Scots eager to break away from the UK government. Some economic **policies** were crippling Scotland, while at the same time allowing businesses in England to prosper. Money from North Sea oil, found in Scottish areas of the sea, was not benefiting most Scots. Many people wanted change.

In September 1997, Scots **voted** for the creation of a Scottish **parliament**. Elections to the parliament took place in May 1999, and it was officially opened by Queen Elizabeth II in July 1999.

Modern Scotland

Since the Scottish parliament was set up in 1999, Scotland has looked to the future with new confidence and pride. Having lost large numbers of people through emigration, Scots are very welcoming to anyone wishing to live and work in Scotland. Many Irish **immigrants** arrived in the 19th century, followed by Italians in the early 1900s. Immigrants from Bangladesh, India, and Pakistan arrived in the late 1900s. Today's immigrants come mainly from eastern Europe. Most Scots, of all backgrounds, feel a very strong loyalty to their local city, town, or region. However, as a whole the people of modern Scotland stand together to take their place in the UK, Europe, and the rest of the world.

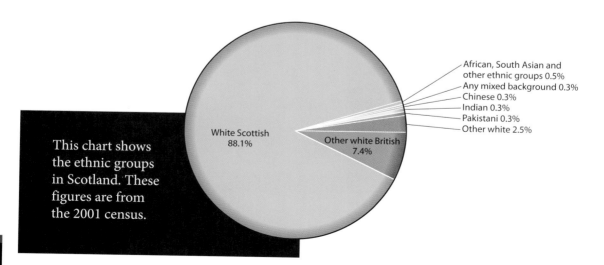

African, South Asian and other ethnic groups 0.5%
Any mixed background 0.3%
Chinese 0.3%
Indian 0.3%
Pakistani 0.3%
Other white 2.5%

White Scottish 88.1%

Other white British 7.4%

This chart shows the ethnic groups in Scotland. These figures are from the 2001 census.

YOUNG PEOPLE

A truly 21st-century sport has come to Scotland! The sport of *parkour*, or "free-running," originally came from France. It involves crossing urban landscapes by vaulting, leaping, and climbing over obstacles. There are growing groups in Aberdeen, Edinburgh, and Glasgow who meet in the cities to train together and practice some really tricky moves!

The T in the Park music festival is an example of Scotland's new modern and vibrant outlook.

Regions and Resources: Land, Industry, and Technology

What is Scotland like? The natural landscape dominates a lot of Scotland, while the **urban** and industrial areas continue to change and grow.

The Highlands and islands

Much of the north and west of Scotland is a mix of mountain and **moorland**. The Grampian Mountains are huge, rounded mountains in the middle of Scotland. These mountains are separated from the northern Highlands by the Great Glen. This is a long line of deep connected lochs (lakes). It is a huge **fault** in the earth's crust. North and west of the Great Glen, more mountains give way to hundreds of islands.

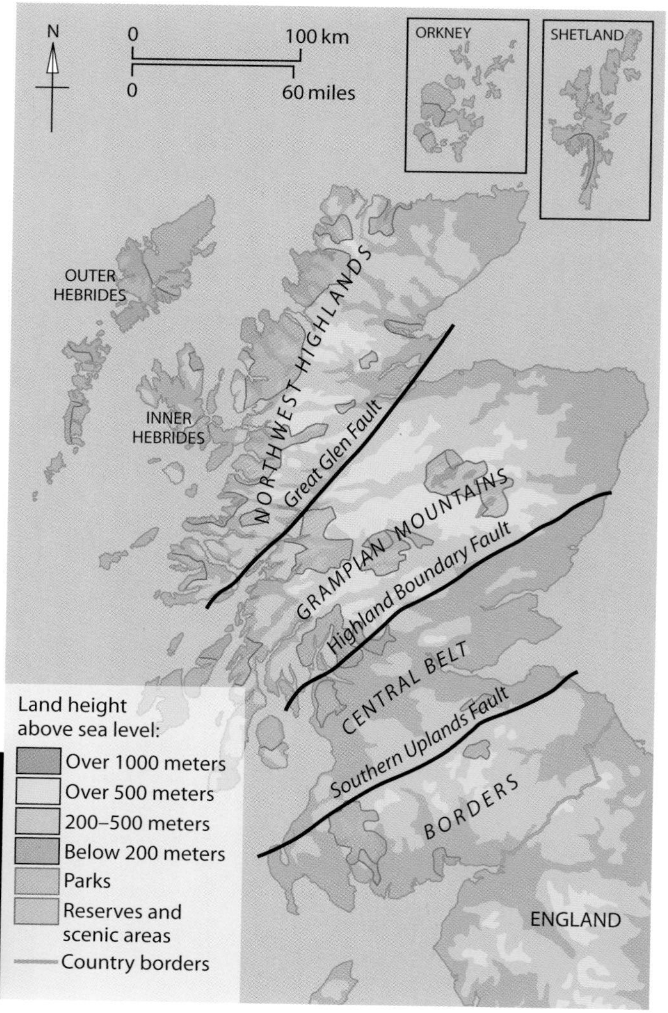

This map shows the **topography** of Scotland and some of the parks and reserves that help to preserve the landscape.

N

| 0 | 100 km |
| 0 | 60 miles |

ORKNEY

SHETLAND

OUTER HEBRIDES

NORTH WEST HIGHLANDS

Great Glen Fault

INNER HEBRIDES

GRAMPIAN MOUNTAINS

Highland Boundary Fault

CENTRAL BELT

Southern Uplands Fault

BORDERS

ENGLAND

Land height above sea level:

- Over 1000 meters
- Over 500 meters
- 200–500 meters
- Below 200 meters
- Parks
- Reserves and scenic areas
- Country borders

The Great Glen is a spectacular and ancient feature of the Scottish landscape.

The Central Belt and Lowlands

The Central Belt lies south of the Highland Boundary Fault, which separates the Highlands from the Lowlands. This region is densely populated and includes Glasgow and Edinburgh, Scotland's largest cities. Most of Scotland's farming and industry is located here.

The Borders and Dumfries & Galloway lie south of the Southern Upland Fault. As the name suggests, the Borders region forms part of the border with England. It is a hilly region with market towns dotted across the landscape.

Daily life

Students living on the tiny island of Papa Westray in northern Scotland usually catch a ferry every day. This takes them to school on the neighboring island of Westray. However, for a few months in 2009 their ferry could not make the journey. The solution? The children traveled to school on the world's shortest flight! The flight, about 1 mile (1.6 kilometers), takes just over one minute!

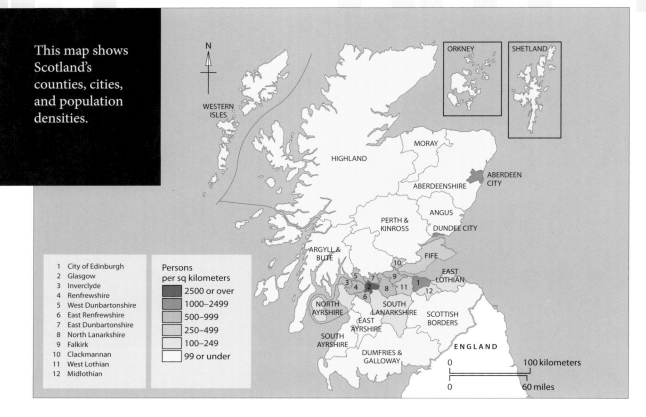

This map shows Scotland's counties, cities, and population densities.

Persons per sq kilometers

- 2500 or over
- 1000–2499
- 500–999
- 250–499
- 100–249
- 99 or under

1. City of Edinburgh
2. Glasgow
3. Inverclyde
4. Renfrewshire
5. West Dunbartonshire
6. East Renfrewshire
7. East Dunbartonshire
8. North Lanarkshire
9. Falkirk
10. Clackmannan
11. West Lothian
12. Midlothian

WESTERN ISLES · HIGHLAND · MORAY · ORKNEY · SHETLAND · ABERDEENSHIRE · ABERDEEN CITY · ANGUS · PERTH & KINROSS · DUNDEE CITY · ARGYLL & BUTE · FIFE · EAST LOTHIAN · NORTH AYRSHIRE · SOUTH LANARKSHIRE · SCOTTISH BORDERS · EAST AYRSHIRE · SOUTH AYRSHIRE · DUMFRIES & GALLOWAY · ENGLAND

0   100 kilometers

0   60 miles

People, places, and jobs

Scotland's total land area is 30,414 square miles (78,772 square kilometers). The population is just over 5 million. There are huge differences in **population densities** across Scotland. Very few people live in the remote Highlands, and some islands are uninhabited. The cities are as densely populated as any modern city, with over 1,000 people per square mile.

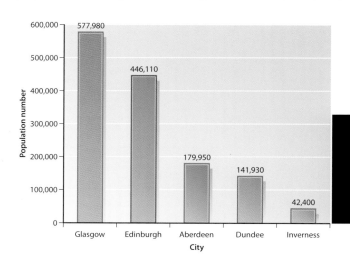

This bar chart shows the populations of Scotland's five biggest cities.

City	Population number
Glasgow	577,980
Edinburgh	446,110
Aberdeen	179,950
Dundee	141,930
Inverness	42,400

Using resources

Scotland's landscape makes it ideal for agriculture, forestry, and fishing. Large areas are farmed for cereals, rapeseed, fruit, and vegetables. Beef cattle, dairy cattle, and sheep are raised on pastureland. Fishing is still big business, especially since the growth of fish farming. Forestry is another industry that shapes much of the landscape. However, only a few people are employed in these industries, because much of the work is done by machinery.

Declining industries

Traditional manufacturing industries are gradually employing fewer people. Shipbuilding was once a huge industry, but it has been in decline since World War II. The historic **textile** industry still produces large amounts of cloth, but has lost many workers due to mechanization. Mining and quarrying have declined, because it is now cheaper to **import** minerals from elsewhere.

The oil and gas industry in the North Sea has brought money and jobs to Scotland since the 1970s. However, the reserves will run out, perhaps as soon as 2020. Scotland will still be able to produce energy from other sources though, for example wave power, so the energy industry looks promising for Scotland.

Scotland's 21st-century economy

Many old, heavy industries in Scotland have now been replaced by new ideas, new businesses, and new jobs. The government is now promoting certain industries. After the global economic problems that began in 2008, Scotland's **unemployment** rate rose slightly to around eight percent. Investment in the following growing industries will give Scotland and its population good reason to feel positive about the future:

- **Life sciences:** Life sciences include biotechnology, which is using living things to improve human health and the environment.

- **Finance and services:** This includes the many call centers in Scotland. Apparently people trust a Scottish accent!

- **Computing and electronics:** This growing industry gave rise to the name "Silicon Glen," an area in the Central Belt where many businesses have set up.

- **Energy:** There is a large focus on developing new technologies for **renewable energy.**

- **Creative industries:** This exciting area includes fashion, design, advertising, film, performing arts, publishing, and music.

- **Tourism and outdoor pursuits:** This will build upon Scotland's existing reputation as an excellent tourist destination.

- **Universities:** Cutting-edge university research is attracting many students and **investors** into Scotland.

DOLLY THE SHEEP

Dolly the Sheep, born in July 1996, was the first living mammal to be **cloned.** She was created at a biotechnology research institute near Edinburgh. She had four lambs. Dolly died in 2003, and her remains are on show at the Royal Museum of Scotland in Edinburgh.

These cyclists are competing in the 2008 Mountain Bike World Cup, at the Nevis Range near Fort William.

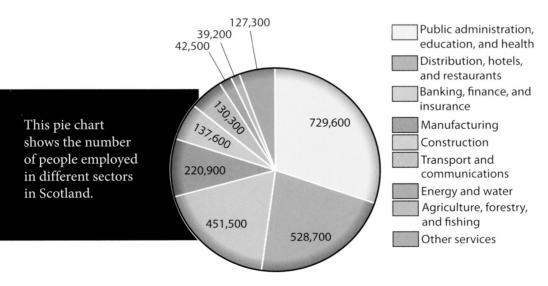

This pie chart shows the number of people employed in different sectors in Scotland.

127,300
39,200
42,500
130,300
137,600
220,900
451,500
528,700
729,600

Public administration, education, and health
Distribution, hotels, and restaurants
Banking, finance, and insurance
Manufacturing
Construction
Transport and communications
Energy and water
Agriculture, forestry, and fishing
Other services

Wildlife: A Precious Resource

Is Scotland's environment a precious resource? At first glance, large areas seem to be fairly empty of life. But look a bit closer . . .

The disappearing forest

Up until about 2,000 years ago, most of Scotland was forested with beech, oak, ash, rowan, birch, and pine. Today only small pockets of this **primeval** forest remain. Large areas were cleared for fuel, timber, and grazing, leaving behind the **heathland** that we see today.

Much of the heathland is covered in heather, which produces a carpet of pink and purple flowers in late summer. In May yellow gorse flowers take their turn. Many insect-eating plants live in damp areas like **peat boglands**. Alpine plants and rare mosses and lichens grow well in the high, rocky, mountainous areas.

Pink and purple heather flowers make a beautiful carpet over the mountains.

Thickly planted forests harm wildlife, destroying their natural habitat.

New forests

Huge **plantations** of conifers were created on poor land from the 1950s onward, to provide softwood timber. The problem with these forests is that very little light reaches the forest floor, so no plants can grow underneath, and very few animals can live there. However, all new plantations must now be managed, so that a more diverse range of plants and animals can flourish there.

How to say...

Gaelic:	forest	*coille*
	heather	*fraoch*
Scots:	stone	*stane*
	lake	*loch*
	valley	*glen*
	cold, wet weather	*dreich*
	stream	*burn*
	hill	*brae*

A haven for wildlife

Scotland's vast areas of uninhabited land have provided a home for many different animals for hundreds of years. However, some **species**, for example wolves and wild boar, have been hunted to **extinction**. Today the threats to wildlife are habitat change, for example bogs being drained for farmland. But there is still much to see, with some patience and a bit of knowledge!

Red deer are the largest type of deer found in the United Kingdom.

Huge herds of deer roam the Highlands and moorlands. Pine martens and **endangered**, secretive wildcats live in forested areas. Sleek otters play around the coastline, and red squirrels thrive in the Highlands. Bird spotters will find capercaillie, ptarmigan, golden eagles, and the rare and endangered corncrake.

Cows, sheep, and ponies

Scotland also has some native domestic animals, which are a bit easier to find! Soay sheep, originally from the island of St. Kilda, have soft brown wool. Aberdeen Angus cattle have beautiful black coats and are raised for beef. Highland cattle are a favorite symbol of Scotland, with their shaggy brown coats and long horns. The tiny Shetland ponies and slightly larger Eriskay ponies are hardy enough to survive harsh Scottish winters outside.

Should wolves be reintroduced?

Wolves became extinct in Scotland in the 1700s. Many people are now campaigning for them to be reintroduced. This would help to keep deer numbers down, so that delicate **ecosystems** damaged by large deer herds would recover. However, opponents fear that wolves would also prey on farm animals, and estate owners would lose money, as there would be less **deer stalking**. What do you think?

This is a Scottish wildcat. Wildcats are much bigger than house cats.

The coast and the sea

Scotland's coast is dotted with around 790 islands. Most are found off the north and west coasts. There are three main groups:

- Northern Isles—includes Shetland and Orkney
- Outer Hebrides—includes Lewis and Harris
- Inner Hebrides—includes Skye, Mull, and Iona.

Most of the islands are **uninhabited**. Many have glorious, white sandy beaches, while others have steep sea cliffs. The coast of the Outer Hebrides is dominated by machair. This is one of the rarest habitats in Europe. Machair is made from shell sand. Beautiful wildflowers such as wild thyme thrive there. The pristine environment attracts many tourists. A fine balance must be kept, so the tourists don't harm the very habitat they have come to see. Some areas are also being affected by **erosion**.

These volunteers are helping to clear trash from a beach in southwest Scotland.

Beautiful wildflowers grow on machair at Balranald reserve in the Outer Hebrides.

Bird life and sea life

Many internationally important **migrating** birds visit Scotland's coastal areas. Puffins, skuas, gannets, guillemots, fulmars, and shearwaters are among the visitors. The seas are also full of life. Bottlenose dolphins, orcas, humpback whales, common and gray seals, and porpoises are commonly seen around the coast.

In recent years, some sea life has been affected by pollution from salmon fish farms. These provide an important source of salmon, as wild salmon is becoming endangered. However, many fish farms are now trying to reduce their impact. The biggest threat to sea life comes from garbage. Hundreds of animals die every year after mistaking plastic bags for food and eating them.

It is clear that Scotland's wildlife and environment are unique and very precious.

Infrastructure: Scotland's Systems

The Scottish Parliament was established in 1999. It can make policies in certain areas. These include:

- agriculture
- education
- environment
- forestry and fishing
- health
- sports and the arts
- tourism and economic development.

Other policies, for example in defense, foreign policy, and social security, can only be dealt with by the UK Parliament. There are 129 members of the Scottish Parliament (MSPs), and they are elected by the Scottish people every four years. Thirty-five percent of them are women. The Scottish Government is made up of members of the winning political party. In 2010, the Scottish National Party (SNP) formed the government, with Alex Salmond at the head as first minister, and Nicola Sturgeon as his deputy.

A healthy nation?

Health care in Scotland is provided by NHS Scotland. It is free and available to everyone. The total running cost is around $18.2 billion (2010), and it is paid for by the **taxes** that people pay. Around half the cost is spent running Scotland's hospitals.

Compared to the rest of the UK, the health of the Scottish people has been poor over the last few decades. This has been due to high levels of smoking and drinking alcohol, and to an unhealthy diet. However, Scotland's health agencies are working hard to improve the nation's health.

This is the debating chamber inside the Scottish Parliament building.

Scottish health statistics		
Life expectancy	75 (men)	80 (women)
Obesity rate	25% (men)	26% (women)
New cases of cancer per year	26,000	
Deaths from cancer per year	15,000	

A literate country

Scotland has been very proud of its education system since the 1500s. This is when the Scottish Church decided to spread education across the whole country. Scotland has many top universities that attract students from all over the world.

Children go to elementary school from the age of five. When they are 12, they go to high school. They must remain at school until they are at least 16. Most schools have a uniform, with a summer version and a winter version. The school day usually starts around 9 a.m. and ends around 3 p.m. for elementary schools, and 4 p.m. for high schools.

Daily life

Some of the elementary schools on Scotland's islands, for example, Canna, are tiny. There is only one classroom, and often only one teacher who is also the school principal.

At the school on the tiny island of Canna there are only two students and one teacher!

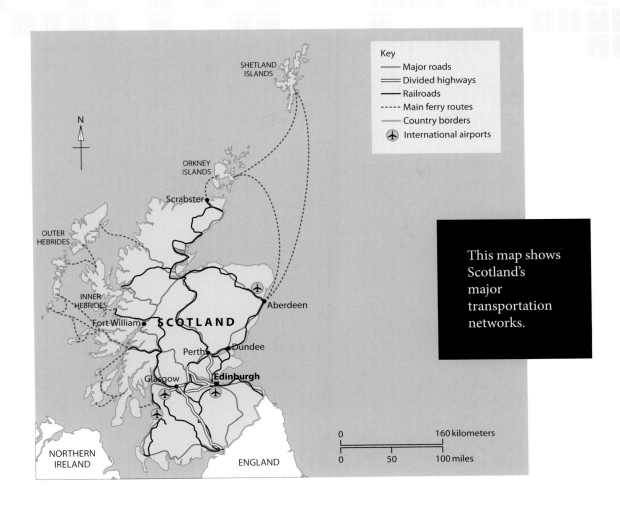

Key
—— Major roads
═══ Divided highways
▬▬ Railroads
----- Main ferry routes
—— Country borders
✈ International airports

This map shows Scotland's major transportation networks.

SHETLAND ISLANDS

ORKNEY ISLANDS

Scrabster

OUTER HEBRIDES

INNER HEBRIDES

Fort William

SCOTLAND

Aberdeen

Perth Dundee

Glasgow Edinburgh

NORTHERN IRELAND

ENGLAND

0   160 kilometers

0   50   100 miles

Road, rail, air, and sea travel

Scotland has a good road network, with some highways. One runs right through Glasgow! The road network is much simpler in the Highlands and islands. This is because the lower population means fewer car journeys, and because there are many mountains and lochs in the way. Scotland has a well-developed railroad network. Glasgow also has a subway (underground train), and a new tram network will run in Edinburgh from 2012.

Transport to and from the islands of Scotland is mainly by ferry. Sometimes the weather means people are stranded for a day or two. Some islands are linked by air travel using ten small airports. At Barra airport, the runway is the beach. There are also four international airports linking Scotland with the rest of the UK, Europe, and the world.

Culture: The Flavor of Scotland

Music in Scotland is very diverse. Traditional **ballads** and songs are still sung. Dances known as jigs and reels set the toes tapping, and bagpipes are the iconic Scottish sound. Many internationally famous bands and singers are Scottish. These include Texas, Travis, Franz Ferdinand, KT Tunstall, Amy Macdonald, and Paulo Nutini.

YOUNG PEOPLE

Many people today think a *ceilidh* is a night of traditional Scottish country dancing. While this is true, more traditional *ceilidhs* include singing, poetry, and music. Everyone is welcome to take the floor!

Words and pictures

Robert Burns is perhaps Scotland's most famous writer. His poems and songs are legendary—one of the most famous is called "Address to a Haggis"! Other writers include Sir Walter Scott, Robert Louis Stevenson, and Muriel Spark. Spark's best-known book is *The Prime of Miss Jean Brodie*. Modern writers include Ian Rankin and Irvine Welsh. The current British **poet laureate** is Carol Ann Duffy, who was born in Glasgow.

Charles Rennie Mackintosh was an artist, designer, and architect. He liked simple lines and floral motifs, and his style has inspired designs for buildings, furniture, jewelry, and art.

How to say...

Gaelic:	music	ceòl
	reel (a type of dance)	righil
Scots:	child	bairn
	drink of whisky	dram
	small	wee
	to chat	blether
	careful	canny
	grumpy	crabbit
	dripping wet	drookit

JACK VETTRIANO (BORN 1951)

One of Scotland and the UK's most popular artists is Jack Vettriano. He was born in Fife, and used to be a mining engineer. His most famous painting, *The Singing Butler*, is the most popular art print in the UK. The painting sold for over $1 million at auction in 2004.

Vettriano's *The Singing Butler* is perhaps the most popular painting in the UK.

A world-class city

Edinburgh is the capital city of Scotland. It is a beautiful, historic city, with a vibrant feel. Fashionable bars and restaurants and modern offices nestle among ancient buildings, monuments, and churches. The center is dominated by the wonderful Edinburgh Castle.

New Year's Eve (called Hogmanay in Scotland) is an event celebrated far more in Scotland than in the rest of the UK, and perhaps the world! Edinburgh hosts one of the world's best street parties for Hogmanay, with an amazing fireworks display set around the castle.

YOUNG PEOPLE

The Edinburgh Festival and Fringe has grown since 1947 into the greatest cultural festival in the world. Acts include mime, street theater, classical music, comedy, poetry, drama, ballet, opera, and movies. The Military Tattoo is held during Festival time. It is a series of displays by military bands and teams, and is set in the castle's **esplanade**.

Gaelic in Glasgow

An Lòchran is an organization set up to promote Gaelic arts and culture in Glasgow. Gaelic is a **Celtic** language spoken mostly in the Highlands and islands. However, less than two percent of the Scottish population now speak Gaelic, and most of these people speak English first. The Scottish government is trying to keep Gaelic from dying out completely. *An Lòchran* is helping to do that by increasing awareness of the language.

BBC Alba was launched in 2008 to provide Gaelic radio and TV programs. It has been a big success and is certainly helping to keep Gaelic alive. *Alba* is the Gaelic word for Scotland.

Bagpipes are played and fireworks are set off over Edinburgh Castle at the finale of the Military Tattoo.

Sports and leisure

Soccer and rugby are the most-watched sports in Scotland. Glasgow-based soccer teams Rangers and Celtic are infamous for their deep rivalry. Fans have been known to fight and taunt each other with songs, flags, and chants.

Popular participation sports are walking, swimming, soccer, cycling, and **curling**. Golf is popular, and Scotland is known throughout the world as "the home of golf." Scotland has excellent facilities for white-water activities, mountain and road biking, diving, fishing, rock climbing, walking, and mountaineering. In the sport of "Munro Bagging," walkers attempt to climb all of Scotland's 283 Munros, the mountains over 3,000 feet (914 meters). Another unique Scottish sport is shinty. It is a bit like field hockey, but the ball can be airborne, and players can tackle each other!

ISLAM FERUZ
(BORN 1995)

Islam and his family fled Somalia when he was seven, and now live in Scotland. In 2009 he was selected for the Scotland under-17 soccer team. "Since my family and I came to Scotland seven years ago, we have been made to feel very welcome," he said. "It's a great country which is now my home and I will be very proud to wear the Scotland jersey."

This climber is ice climbing up a cliff on Aonoch Moor. Scotland's landscape and winter weather are perfect for this sport!

A sporting anthem

Scotland has no official national anthem, but "Flower of Scotland" has been adopted as the unofficial one. It is sung at many big sporting events. The song is about the Battle of Bannockburn in 1314, when the Scottish army defeated Edward II of England:

> *O Flower of Scotland*
> *When will we see your like again*
> *That fought and died for*
> *Your wee bit hill and glen.*
> *And stood against him,*
> *Proud Edward's army,*
> *And sent him homeward*
> *Tae think again.*

Food and drink

In past years Scotland has developed a reputation for unhealthy food, including deep-fried pizzas! However, modern Scottish cuisine is changing. There is some superb home produce available, including lamb, beef, and game (such as deer). The seafood and fish is delicious.

A national dish

Haggis is a Scottish icon. It is made of sheep heart, liver, and lungs minced with onion, oatmeal, **suet**, spices, and salt. Cranachan is a delicious dessert. It is made with cream, honey, whisky, raspberries, and oatmeal.

Haggis is traditionally served with mashed neeps (turnips) and tatties (potatoes).

Shortbread

Ask an adult to help you make this delicious cookie.

Ingredients

- ½ cup butter
- ¼ cup granulated sugar
- 1 ¾ all-purpose flour

What to do

1. Preheat oven to 375° Fahrenheit (190° Celsius).
2. Beat the butter and sugar together until smooth.
3. Stir in the flour to make a smooth paste. Turn onto a flat surface and gently roll out until the paste is ½ inch (1 centimeter) thick.
4. Cut into rounds or fingers and place onto a baking tray. Chill in the fridge for 20 minutes.
5. Bake in the oven for 15–20 minutes, or until pale golden-brown. Cool on a wire rack.

A national drink

Whisky is another Scottish icon. It is a very alcoholic drink made from a type of grain called barley. The rarest bottles can sell for tens of thousands of dollars.

Irn Bru is a bright-orange, fruit-flavored soft drink that is Scotland's second national drink! It was invented in 1901 and is known for its controversial advertisements.

Scotland Today

Scotland is a small country with a big reputation. Its history and its icons conjure up a wild, romantic land. It is also a thoroughly modern country, whose people have much to be proud of.

A sense of . . . ?

Anyone visiting Scotland will feel the sense of pride in most Scots. The new Scottish parliament has breathed new life into the country. Scots at last feel that their country is important, valued, and a cool place to live. The culture is strong and the landscape is unique. The people are supported by excellent health care and education.

There is also a fabulous sense of humor in most Scots, although sometimes it is not obvious! Scots have a great ability to laugh at themselves, and make jokes about their own thriftiness (being particularly careful about money)!

Scottish energy companies are testing new ways to produce energy without harming the environment. This device on Loch Ness turns wave energy into electricity.

Tourists visit Scotland's capital city, Edinburgh, to experience its beauty, history, and culture.

The 21st century

Scotland is looking forward. New technologies, especially in the energy sector, are leading the world. New people are moving to live and work there. In remote places, the Internet is encouraging people to stay and to set up new online businesses. This is all bringing money and jobs to areas that were once very poor.

Scotland's modern cities are exciting and dynamic. At the same time, they are close enough to mountains, moorland, and the coast to allow people to escape town life. This is perhaps Scotland's biggest appeal—it can offer something for everyone.

Fact File

Official language:	English, two percent also speak Gaelic
Capital city:	Edinburgh
Bordering country:	England
Population:	5.2 million
Birth rate:	10.7 per 1,000 population
Death rate:	11.0 per 1,000 population
Religion:	Presbyterian Kirk (Church) of Scotland: 42% Roman Catholic: 16% Other Christian: 7% No religion: 28% Other religions, the largest of which is Islam: 2% Religion not stated: 5%
National symbols:	The **thistle** is the national flower. It appears on Scottish bank notes. **Tartan** is a popular symbol of Scotland. It comes in many different designs, but the basic pattern is a woven lattice with horizontal and vertical stripes of color.
Flag:	The Saltire, or St. Andrew's Cross. The flag has a blue background with a white diagonal cross. It represents St. Andrew, Scotland's patron saint. It is thought that he was crucified on a cross of this shape.
Area:	30,414 square miles (78,772 square kilometers)

Major rivers:	Tay, 120 miles (193 kilometers) Spey, 106 miles (172 kilometers) Clyde, 106 miles (171 kilometers) Tweed, 97 miles (156 kilometers) Forth, 65 miles (105 kilometers)
Major lochs (lakes):	Lomond, 21 square miles (56 square kilometers) Ness, 21 square miles (56 square kilometers) Awe, 14 square miles (38 square kilometers) Maree, 11 square miles (29 square kilometers)
Highest elevation:	Ben Nevis, 4,409 feet (1,344 meters)
Currency:	Pound sterling. Scottish banks are allowed to print their own notes, so there are four different designs of each note.
Exports:	Food and drink; chemicals; business services; office machinery
Literacy rate:	99 percent of the population can read and write
Inventions:	The modified steam engine, waterproof raincoats, tarmacadam (tarmac), penicillin, telephones, and television
Public holidays:	New Year (January 1 and 2), Good Friday, May Day Bank Holiday, Spring Bank Holiday (last Monday in May), Summer Bank Holiday (first Monday in August), St. Andrew's day (November 30), Christmas Day (December 25), Boxing Day (December 26).

Timeline

CE is short for Common Era. CE is added after a date and means that the date occurred after the birth of Jesus Christ, for example, 720 CE.

80–84 CE	The Roman General Agricola invades Caledonia (the Roman word for Scotland)
142 CE	The Roman emperor Antonine builds a defensive wall across the narrowest part of Caledonia, between the rivers Clyde and Forth
170 CE	The Romans retreat back to Hadrian's Wall, in northern England, and make no further advances in Caledonia
500s CE	Scotti (Irish **Celts**) invade Scotland's west coast. Anglo-Saxons begin settling in the southeastern part of Scotland.
563 CE	Christianity comes to Scotland as St. Columba, a missionary from Ireland, founds a religious community on the island of Iona
700s CE	Vikings invade
843 CE	Kenneth MacAlpin becomes first king of Scotland
1018	King Malcom II defeats Anglo-Saxons and Scotland is born
1232–1469	Vikings give land back to Scotland
1296	King Edward I of England invades Scotland
1297	William Wallace leads Scotland to victory at Stirling Bridge. King Edward I is defeated.
1305	William Wallace is captured and killed
1314	Robert the Bruce leads Scotland to victory at Bannockburn. King Edward II is defeated.
1500s	The Scottish Reformation shakes religion. The Scottish Church begins a country-wide free education system.
1507	The first printing press arrives in Edinburgh
1560	John Knox founds the Presbyterian **Protestant** religion
1568	The **Catholic** Mary, Queen of Scots, flees Scotland and her baby son, James VI, is raised as a Protestant
1603	King James VI of Scotland also becomes King James I of England, after Elizabeth I of England dies

1660	Charles II is restored as king of England (and Wales), Scotland, and Ireland
1685	Charles II dies, his brother becomes James VII of Scotland (James II of England)
1688	The Protestant Dutch Prince William of Orange overthrows King James
1707	The Treaty of Union is signed and Scotland ceases to be an independent nation. The United Kingdom is created.
1715	The first Jacobite Uprising. Supporters of the old King James want his son, James Edward, to be restored as king. The rebellion fails.
1745	James Edward's son, Charles Edward Stuart (Bonnie Prince Charlie) leads the second Jacobite Uprising
1746	Bonnie Prince Charlie is defeated at Culloden, near Inverness
1700s–1800s	The **Highland Clearances** force many Scots to **emigrate**. The **Industrial Revolution** brings huge advances. Many Irish **immigrants** arrive.
1801	Scotland's population is 1,608,420
1846	A railroad line connects Edinburgh and London
1890	The Forth Railway Bridge is completed
1900s	Immigrants arrive from Italy, Bangladesh, India, and Pakistan
1911	Scotland's population is 4,760,904
1914–1918	World War I. Scotland loses around 100,000 soldiers in the fighting.
1931	Scotland's population begins to decline as people **migrate** to find better jobs
1939–1945	World War II. Areas in Glasgow, Edinburgh, Aberdeen, and Dundee are bombed.
1947	The first Edinburgh Festival is held
1950s	Large-scale conifer planting begins
1976	Large-scale oil production in the North Sea begins
1996	Dolly the Sheep, the first living mammal to be **cloned**, is born
1997	A huge majority of Scots vote "yes" in a referendum on devolution and the creation of a Scottish parliament
May 1999	Elections take place for the new Scottish **Parliament**
July 1999	The Scottish Parliament is officially opened by Queen Elizabeth II
2000s	Immigrants arrive from Eastern Europe
2003	Dolly the sheep dies
2004	The new parliament building at Holyrood in Edinburgh is officially opened
2005	**G8** Summit takes place in Gleneagles Hotel, near Perth, where world leaders meet to discuss global challenges

Glossary

Anglo-Saxon people, originally from Germany, who lived in England before the Norman Conquest in 1066

bagpipes wind instrument made of a leather bag and pipes

ballad poem or song that tells a story

Catholic branch of Christianity that is led by the pope

Celtic to do with the Celts, an ancient group of tribes that lived in Scotland, Ireland, Wales, and parts of Cornwall and northern France

clone create an identical copy using complex scientific methods

culture practices, traditions, and beliefs of a society

curling game played on ice in which two teams slide a stone toward a circle at either end

deer stalking tracking and hunting deer to shoot

economy to do with money and the industry and jobs in a country

ecosystem community of living things

emigrate leave one country to live in another

endangered in danger of extinction

erosion wearing away of the earth's surface by wind, water, or ice

esplanade level, open expanse of pavement

extinction dying out of a species

famine large-scale lack of food over a wide area

fault crack in the rock that makes up the earth's crust

G8 group of the eight richest countries in the world

haggis dish made of sheep or calf organs that are minced, then mixed with suet, oatmeal, and seasonings

heathland open areas of remote land

highland region or area of a country that has many hills or mountains

immigrant person who moves from their native land to live in another country

import buy goods from another country

industrialized affected by many different kinds of industry

Industrial Revolution changes that took place in how goods were made, from small-scale production by people to large factories in which machines did most of the work. The Industrial Revolution began in the late 1700s in England.

investor person or company who puts money into a business

manufacturing making things in large quantities using machines

migrate change habitat or location, usually when the seasons change

moorland area of high land that is covered in low-lying vegetation

noble person of high rank or title

parliament group of people who make the laws for a country

peat bogland wet area with soil that is made up of decayed plants. Peat can be used as a fuel or fertilizer.

plantation large area of land where one type of plant is grown to sell

poet laureate poet honored by royalty and expected to write poems for celebratory occasions and of national significance

policy rule or plan that is used as a guide for action

population density number of people living in a certain area

primeval prehistoric or primitive

Protestant branch of Christianity that is separate from the Catholic or Orthodox church

renewable energy natural source of energy that will never run out, such as solar or wind energy

species type of animal, bird, or fish

suet hard fat from around the kidneys or loins of cattle or sheep

tartan woollen cloth woven into a plaid design

tax money paid by people to the government. Taxes can come from wages or be placed on goods that people buy.

tenant person who occupies or uses another's house, building, office, or land, usually in exchange for rent

textile cloth or fabric

thistle plant with prickly leaves and a head of purple flowers

topography natural and artificial physical features of an area

tribe independent social group, historically often made up of primitive or nomadic people

unemployment percentage of workers that do not have jobs

uninhabited not lived in

urban having to do with a city or a town

vote to choose. People vote for someone to win an election.

Find Out More

Books

Adil, Janeen R. *Scotland: A Question and Answer Book*. Mankato, MN: Capstone Press, 2007.

Levy, Patricia. *Scotland*. New York: Benchmark Books, 2011.

Nardo, Don. *Freedom Fighter: William Wallace and Scotland's Battle for Independence*. Mankato, MN: Compass Point Books, 2010.

Wilson, Barbara Ker. *Stories from Scotland*. New York: Oxford University Press, 2009.

Websites

www.visitscotland.com

Visit the official website of Scotland's national tourism organization. Find out what to do and where to do it. Find accommodation and places to eat. If you want to travel in an eco-friendly way, there is a section on green tourism.

www.visitscotland.org

Look at the business website of Scotland's national tourism organization for statistics and information on Scotland's tourism industry.

www.gro-scotland.gov.uk

Visit the website of the General Register Office for Scotland to look at census data and Scottish family history records.

www.activity-scotland.org.uk

The Activity Scotland Association is an organization that represents providers of activities throughout Scotland. All activity organizations listed on their website must meet strict safety and quality levels.

www.ltscotland.org.uk

Learning and Teaching Scotland is an organization funded by the Scottish government to transform education in Scotland. The "Scotland's History" section contains a wealth of information about Scotland through the ages.

Places to visit

If you ever get the chance to explore Scotland, these organizations can help you plan your visit:

Historic Scotland

This organization is responsible for safeguarding Scotland's historic environment and encourages people to understand and enjoy it. It cares for 345 historic sites, from wreck sites, to ruined castles, to ancient wells.

The National Trust for Scotland

This charity works to protect and promote the natural and cultural heritage of Scotland. It owns St. Kilda, a World Heritage Site, 16 islands, 7 national nature reserves, 26 castles, palaces, and country houses, 4 battle sites, and 35 gardens. Its motto is "A place for everyone."

Scottish Natural Heritage

This organization's job is to encourage people to care for and improve the natural heritage of Scotland. It teaches people how to understand Scottish heritage and enjoy it responsibly. Its motto is "All of nature for all of Scotland."

Topic Tools

You can use these topic tools for your school projects. Trace the map onto a sheet of paper, using the thick black outline to guide you.

The Scottish flag is known as the Saltire. There is a legend that the Scottish king Angus looked up at the blue sky during a battle and saw a white saltire (diagonal cross), and this was the origin of the flag. The flag is also known as St. Andrew's Cross, after St. Andrew, the patron saint of Scotland. Copy the flag design, and then color in your picture. Make sure you use the right colors!

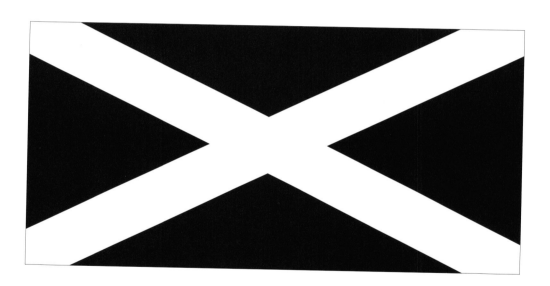

Edinburgh

Index